Cont

Disclaimer

All rights reserved. No part of this book may be reproduced in any form without permission in writing from the author. Reviewers may quote brief passages in reviews.

No part of this publication may be reproduced or transmitted in any form or by any means, mechanical or electronic, including photocopying or recording, or by any information storage and retrieval system, or transmitted by email without permission in writing from the publisher.

While all attempts have been made to verify the information provided in this publication, neither the author nor the publisher assumes any responsibility for errors, omissions or contrary interpretations of the subject matter herein.

Neither the author nor the publisher assumes any responsibility or liability whatsoever on the behalf of the purchaser or the reader of these materials.

Your Gift

As a way of saying *thanks* for purchasing and reading this book, I am giving you a free gift and I invite you to take a look at my   blog   – http://entrepreneurenhanced.com

*To get this gift click on the photo or click on the blog to sign up to my email list.

Introduction

Have you ever wanted to make money online while you are sleeping, while you are travelling or while you are doing things you enjoy?

Have you ever wanted to build an online business which you can manage from anywhere around the world?

Do you have a job from 9 to 5, but you want more money and more freedom?

I think I might know what you want and what you need – a passive income online business. You can start doing this by creating websites which promote products from Amazon (Amazon Associates), you can start a self-publishing business through Amazon (KDP – Kindle Direct Publishing) or you can create your own private label products and sell them on Amazon (Amazon FBA).

More and more people are starting online businesses and are trying to get into the so-called "Internet Lifestyle". To achieve this, you need to set up multiple online businesses.

You know what they say, don't keep all your eggs in one basket. The same principle is applied in online businesses – you never know when one of them will collapse.

If you are trying to do the same, this book is a good place to start from, it is an excellent way to start your future online career.

This book will guide you to create websites and to make money from them through Amazon's Affiliate program which is called Amazon Associates. In this book I have covered:

- *What is affiliate marketing and how it works*
- *How to create a website (niche website or authority website)*
- *How to sign up with Amazon*
- *How to sign up with Wordpress*
- *How to pick a niche topic*
- *How much money you can make*
- *How much money you need to invest*
- *What products to promote*
- *What is an Amazon aStore*
- *Tips*
- *Things you have to avoid on Amazon*
- *SEO basics*
- *Why Social Media is important for any business*
- *What you need to build an email list*

Before we get right into the subject, I want to thank you for purchasing the book, and I congratulate you for taking action. There are people who always comment and talk uselessly, and there are few people who want to try out something new and make money on their own.

You are on the right path.

Chapter 1: Introduction to Amazon Associates Program and Affiliate Marketing

What is Affiliate Marketing?

I am quite sure that you have seen tons of ads all over the internet which sometimes become really annoying, but some of them get your attention, and you get to click on them. Behind these ads there is always somebody hiding – there is somebody who is promoting products, either if they are digital or physical ones.

This advertising method which consists of ads and links to products on different platforms is called **Affiliate Marketing.**

Basically, all of the big companies offer affiliate partnerships with people like you and me who want to earn money online, passively.

Through Affiliate Marketing you promote products and whenever a customer purchases a product through your affiliate links you will get a commission between 4 and 10% (on Amazon, on other platforms it can go up to 50%).

What is Amazon Associates?

Amazon Associates is Amazon's own affiliate program – anyone can join it and can generate money using Amazon huge platform. You can promote any kind of product on Amazon – books, physical products, digital products (Kindle books), video games, clothes, electronics, laptops, headphones, etc.

How much money can you earn trough Amazon Associates?

The potential is unlimited, it's totally up to you how much money you want to generate and how motivated you are. It requires a lot of work and dedication, even though it's a relatively easy process, and it can generate money passively on auto-pilot.

Where do you promote these products?

No matter what products you need to promote, you will need an online place which has a lot of monthly traffic. These places can be websites, YouTube videos, a blog, a Facebook fan page (personal or for specific products), even digital books. It can literally be any kind of place where people come, the more places you put affiliate links, the more money you will be making.

Why should you go for Affiliate Marketing with Amazon Associates?

Everybody wants to get more money as fast as possible, and Affiliate Marketing is one of the fastest ways to get started making money online.

The main advantages of Affiliate Marketing is that it's an online income stream and if you have another job or you don't have time to keep an eye on your Affiliate Marketing business, don't worry, it will make you money even when you sleep.

Here's why you should go for Affiliate Marketing:

1. *Fast to start* – You can find a niche and create a website in a couple of

days, and you can begin making money.

2. ***Cheap to start*** – you need less than $100 to start and finish a website which can bring you ten times more each month once it's finished.

3. ***Easy learning curve*** – you will get familiar with the whole process in less than 1 month if you are constantly focusing.

4. ***Passive income stream*** – once you finish a website/online place, and you optimize it, you are 99% done – it will make you money all the time. I am saying 99% because the other 1% represents the keywords which are constantly changing – trends are changing, products are changing, competition is growing and you should

keep an eye on your websites and optimize them occasionally.

5. ***Easy to maintain*** – it's quite easy to manage Affiliate Websites – 99% of your work is already done, all you have to do is to keep an eye on your sales and try to optimize it constantly (keywords, products, links etc.)

6. ***Flexibility*** – you can work at any time, from any place that you want – at home, at a coffee shop, while travelling.

Can you make a living out of Affiliate Marketing?

Yes, indeed. Affiliate Marketing is everywhere, it's constantly growing and it will never disappear – more and more people are buying stuff online – it's cheaper, faster, more comfortable and most of them offer refunds as well. As real stores are expensive to maintain – rent, employees, profit, utilities, etc. the online market has seemed to be the perfect way to expand any kind of business.

Any business needs promotion – and here comes the magic with Affiliate Marketing. You can make a good living out of it if you work hard and create the best websites on the best niches. Some of them are more profitable, some of them are less, but the truth is that it is cheap to start, and it will definitely be worth giving a try for any kind of niche. I will discuss more about picking the right niche in the next chapter.

Before you start this kind of business or any other business which involves Amazon – Kindle Direct Publishing (KDB) or Fulfillment By Amazon (FBA) – you will not get rich overnight.

If you want to start a business as an Amazon Affiliate, be aware that you have to put serious work into, and you have to invest time, money and skill to obtain decent profits.

I will cover up next what you need to do and where you can find the resources you need to get started as fast as possible.

Chapter 2: How to pick a profitable niche – tools and tips

The first thing you have to consider when you start building your Affiliate Marketing business is to decide what kind of products you are going to promote and what kind of websites that you are going to create.

There are 3 main types of websites that you want to go for:

1. ***Niche websites*** – small websites which only target a small market of products – examples – car accessories, laptops, headphones, smartphones, tablets, etc. While "Electronics" is a broad niche, tablets will be a narrower one – a niche.

2. *Authority websites* – bigger websites which promote few categories of products – they include several niches.

3. *Blog* – here you can create a personal blog with what you like, hobbies, thoughts, news, reviews, etc. and for each section you can add Affiliate Links. For example, if you enjoy running – after you create an article about running you can then make a short list of products to promote – running shoes, running gear, etc.

The best way to succeed in affiliate marketing is to create all of them – create a blog, an authority website (or more) and dozens of niche websites. Then what you want is to promote them and an essential way to do this and maximize traffic is to cross promote them – niche site A promotes niche site B. Niche site B promote niche site C. Niche site C promotes niche site C. The authority website can promote niche sites A, B, C, D. Your blog can promote your authority website. Your niche sites can link your blog and so on – create a web of links to promote all of your websites.

You will basically get different traffic for all of them, and you will send the traffic from A to B to C to D to the authority website, to the blog and vice-versa.

You won't send all your traffic from each one of them to the other ones, but a certain percentage of the overall traffic for one niche site will get to the other websites that you create.

How do you know which niche sells?

The internet now offers you a lot of tools to get started – you will know from the beginning how much traffic a keyword gets, how much competition you get and the average sales that you will make through a niche.

You need to take into consideration a few things before you go for a niche:

1. *How much competition the niche has*
2. *How much searches the niche gets (monthly searches in average)*
3. *How many products can you promote for that niche*
4. *If you are passionate about that niche (it's important)*
5. *If the niche will be a long term one*

To get started, you will need a keyword tool and the one which I recommend is Google's Keyword Planner.

To access it, go to Google.com and type in the search bar "Google Keyword Planner". You will see then Google AdWords and

Google Keyword Planner at the "Tools" section.

For example, if you are passionate about hunting, you can create a hunting website, and you can promote hunting products – hunting knives, bows, equipment, accessories, etc.

For the keyword hunting knife – you will get different results using Google Keyword tool:

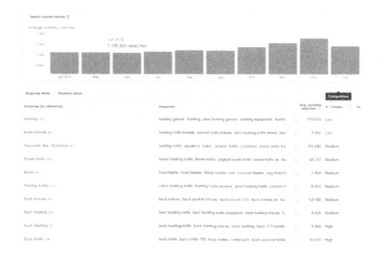

By using this tool, you will be able to see how many people are searching for that keyword each month and how much competition you have for that niche.

You have to understand that you can make a lot of money from $200 to $1000 for each website that you create if you choose the right niche. Don't pick broad niche such as "Poker", "Electronics", "Apple", etc. – you just can't stand a change in front of the major competitors who have a history, a large website (authority website).

For such keywords, the competition is so high, that you won't see a penny.

All you need is a niche which is not so common, it has 1,000 – 5,000 searches monthly (in average) and which has a low competition. Like in the picture above, you can clearly see that there are a number of searches, the competition level, and the keywords.

What you will need to know further is to optimize you niche website using Search Engine Optimization (SEO) which I will also discuss.

Chapter 3: Signing up with WordPress and getting started with your website

Before you can sign up with the Amazon Associates program, you need to create a website and get a domain. The best platform for the purpose of your websites (affiliate marketing) is WordPress.

You should avoid the mistake I've done at the beginning – I signed up with WordPress.com, I purchased a custom theme and I eventually found out that their .com plan is just for blogging.

Even if I have a blog myself, you are not allowed to create an email list, to do affiliate marketing and you can't install any other plugins either. In other words, you need the WordPress.org platform (go to a hosting platform, purchase hosting and a domain and then login and install WordPress).

When I was talking about customizing you website, I was referring to use custom designs from WordPress, which are coded and ready to go.

In case you want a 100% custom design, prepare to pay hundreds of dollars for the custom design + custom coding. Then you have to install Wordpress plugins and optimize it. It's a little bit more complicated, so in case you are a beginner, I highly recommend to go with WordPress custom designs and choose the one you like the most.

Build a website using WordPress and customize it wisely so it will look professional and it will attract a lot of people (traffic). The more traffic you get, the more sales you will get from your future affiliate links.

Get a domain name and a hosting service. You can get domains from and full web hosting from:

- ***BlueHost***
- ***GoDaddy***
- ***HostGator***
- ***DreamHost***

I recommend BlueHost as it's affordable, it delivers great quality, and it's also specially optimized for WordPress. BlueHost is the web hosting platform that I am using. If you sign up with them, you also get a free domain name and dozens of other advantages.

Prices for hosting vary – you can pay from $4 a month (or $28-$30/ year) to $100 / year for premium quality and priority support.

Of course, you can get a domain from a place and web hosting from another place in case you want everything custom and the best quality for your website.

As your goal is to create Affiliate Niche websites, you want everything to be done fast, so you should get the domain and web hosting service from the same place – try BlueHost, it's the best choice for Affiliate Marketing and for WordPress websites.

Chapter 4: How to create your content for your websites

The content that you are about to create will be crucial for your future Affiliate Marketing business. Now it depends on what kind of website you create – an Authority website, a niche website or a blog.

For niche websites, you will need from 5 to 20 web pages (even more if you may like), and you can get them done in multiple ways:

- Write it by yourself (it will take longer)
- Hire a freelancer from http://freelancer.com or http://odesk.com
- Hire a Ghostwriter from http://iWriter.com

- Hire a virtual assistant and tell him what to write and what to do

Your pages need to be about the keyword (niche) that you have chosen.

For our last example – hunting knife or hunting in general – you can write about the best hunting knives (2 pages) – 3-4 reviews about some hunting knives that you think are excellent quality (4 pages), you can write about how to maintain a hunting knife (how to sharpen it, how to keep it safe etc.) – 2 pages, you can make a page with tips and tricks for hunting knives – 1-2 pages, you can make a list where you can go hunting, etc. – you have dozens of subjects to write about hunting, hunting knives, etc. and for each product that you review/promote – acquire affiliate links from Amazon.

Before creating an account on Amazon, you will need to figure out what content you create and which products you are going to promote on your website.

Of course, this is just an example, you can go for any niche that you desire. Remember what I have told you from the previous chapters, try to promote something that you are passionate about. It will be a lot easier to understand, promote and write about things that you know and love.

For example, if you would choose to promote tablets, or headphones or some electronics (a niche) you can make reviews, unboxings, comparisons, tips and include links from YouTube. Think what's best to use on your niche website that will attract potential customers.

If you choose to pay for all these web pages, product reviews, ideas, tricks, etc. you will need to pay somewhere around $10 / page so you will invest around $100 in the content. If you have enough time to do it yourself, then go for it, but I think it's best to outsource this and hire somebody else to do this job while you focus on other tasks.

For Authority websites, you can also outsource content and hire writers or virtual assistants, but it will be a lot more work to put in, and it will also be a lot more expensive.

The Authority website can be built on the go, you can't come up with 100 pages at a glance, you will need to figure out what you will talk about, what you will be promoting and what audience you are targeting.

Before you build an Authority website (+100 web pages), you should focus on creating multiple Niche website to generate a decent amount of money from the products that you promote as an affiliate.

On the other hand, a blog is really important to build in parallel with your niche websites.

Remember the cross promotion method: every niche website, authority website or blog that you own should promote 1-2 other websites that you have, so the traffic from A goes to B, the traffic from B goes to C and so on. You have big chances of maximizing your profits.

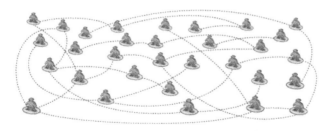

As soon as you get your content, arrange everything in such a manner, so your website looks clean and professional.

You can also include YouTube videos, tutorials, funny videos, etc. and you can also create your own videos and advertise the website and the product and get more traffic.

I will discuss more about social media marketing in the upcoming chapters.

It's very important to make a plan before you start doing everything I have told you, I advise you to do them in the order that I have presented them.

After you are done with creating your content for niche websites, you will need to optimize your website using SEO.

I will cover up what you need to know about SEO, and then we'll discuss about starting your account with Amazon Associates and a few marketing strategies.

Chapter 5: Optimizing your websites using Search Engine Optimization (SEO) – the basics

SEO – Search Engine Optimization is crucial for your future website and for your future sales. It will help you rank your website over other websites and get exposure – if it's used correctly, you will obtain maximum profits out of your websites.

I will cover up the basics of SEO which you need to know when you get started (or before you get started).

When you think at SEO, you have to think of Google's search engines – how and what can you do to rank higher? What can you do in such manner that people will find you easier when they type a certain keyword? Using the right SEO tools is the answer.

Google has a lot of algorithms for which it ranks websites – the keyword for which you try to rank, the number of times the keyword appears on your website (page), if your content is relevant to the keywords, if you are using social media platforms, if you are using the correct links, if your website appears on other bigger websites or related websites, if your website is recommended or shared by people, etc.

These days, SEO is a real challenge for marketers to optimize their website as well as possible to obtain the best profits. Here is a short list of what you have to keep in mind:

1. *Keyword research* – this is the most important thing about SEO – you

need to find out the best keywords for the niche website or any other kind of website that you are building. In case you picked the wrong keyword, but you have optimized everything correctly, you can have the surprise to rank for… nothing… or for something else. Before you start ranking for some keywords, you need to know how much traffic that keyword gets, how much is the PPC (Google Adwords) and how much competition you have – knowing these you will know what to expect.

2. *Use Keyword analyzers* – use Google Adwords (keyword planner, there is an example above in the previous chapters), SEObook keyword planner or any other planner to see everything clearly about the market that you want to enter.

3. *Social Media Platforms* – create platforms for your website on Google+, Facebook, Pinterest, Twitter, LinkedIn and wherever you can – the more people see your website/links to the website, the more exposure you will get – the more traffic you will get. I am sure you didn't know that it really matters for Google if you get Facebook Shares, comments, reviews, tweets or if you have any activity on any other platforms – Google will see, and it will rank you higher.

4. *Backlinks* – it's really important to build backlinks for your website – send traffic to other websites or to products of your own. Optimize everything correctly.

5. *Keep everything you create relevant* – if your content is irrelevant or it has a keyword which appears too many times, Google will penalize you.

6. *Build several websites which promotes each other with backlinks* – it's important to have more than just 1 website to promote different kind of products (different niches). If you want to dominate the market and to become an Authority, build several related websites on the same niche and relate between them.

7. *Use clean URLs* – when you are on-page-SEO, make sure that your URL link is clean, Google likes clean URLs and so do customers.

8. *Duplicate content* – put several pages with similar pages (but NOT identical!!) – this will increase your ranking.

9. *Keep up to date with Google* – as you know, Google always updates its algorithms, and you will have an advantage over other competitors if you know everything in advance.

This is just a short summary of what you need to know about SEO. I highly recommend to check out tutorials, YouTube videos or to buy professional courses for expert SEO.

It is the main piece of your success in affiliate marketing, website building, blogging and any other form of online success.

Chapter 6: Using Social Media for additional traffic and advertising

Social Media is one of the keys to every marketer's success. I haven't seen a successful blog or website without having links to Facebook, Pinterest, Twitter, and YouTube.

The reason why everybody uses them is that you get a lot more exposure, traffic, and you can increase your website's rank (SEO) and you will get more and more people to click on your affiliate links.

Every website that you will create should have something like this:

Also, you can create Facebook Fan pages for every niche website that you create and for your blog. Send your traffic from one to another for the best performance.

Imagine that when you request a new link from Amazon, you can put it on all your Facebook Pages, you can tweet them, share them and get the ultimate exposure.

Let me give you an example – if you decide to create a niche website about wilderness extreme survival – you create a niche website with place where you can go, the wildest places on earth, the best techniques which you can learn, make review of different objects (hunting knives, tents, boots etc.) and when you request a new affiliate link for an object (for example a hammac with mosquito nets) and you can write on all your Social Media platforms something like – *"A new hammac with mosquito nets has been released and is available for purchase. It has XX features, it can support XX weight, it's made of XX material and it's guaranteed to last XX (make a short review and introduction). For those who are interested please check the link below – affiliate link"*.

If you have Fan Pages plus other Social Media accounts, you will definitely find somebody to click on your affiliate links. Imagine if you manage to build 4-5 Fan

Pages with over 100,000 likes and followers. For every link that you put there, at least 5,000 will click on it and at least 100 will buy something through your affiliate links (it varies). This transforms into a 2% conversion rate, which means that 2% of the people who clicked on your affiliate link bought something.

As you may know, if they click on the hammac but they buy a hunting knife or any other product through your link within 24 hours, you will get a commission.

Also, remember that if there is a person who liked what you are doing, he/she will share your page (or pages), and you will get additional exposure. Not everybody will follow you and not everybody will like what you are doing, but there will always be someone who likes what you are doing.

You should probably be aware of the traffic which is present on Social Media to have an idea of the massive potential:

Don't forget about YouTube and Google+, they are extremely powerful. On Google+ you can +1 your posts, share them with the world and get additional traffic.

On YouTube, you have 3 possibilities:

1. *Create reviews for products.*
2. *Film yourself about different topics.*
3. *Make tutorials of what you do.*

In the description of each video, you will need to put links to Facebook, Pinterest, Twitter and all the other platforms that you use, the affiliate links and the link to your blog. In this way, you will send traffic from YouTube to your affiliate products and to your Social Media platforms. From the Social Media platforms, you will send a small percentage to your other affiliate links and generate sales. Even if you make more traffic but don't make too many sales, don't worry, you will get a better rank in SEO, and you will get additional exposure. Whatever you do, you will get a benefit.

Remember, Social Media is essential for any kind of business or website that you are willing to build.

Chapter 7: Create an email list from your niche websites

This is one of the most important steps that you have to take into consideration after you finish your niche websites.

An email list is the best way to keep in touch with all your customers and the people that arrive on your website.

To build an effective email list you need:

1. *A squeeze page* – the place where your customers will write down their email. You will need some nice buttons, a text which will convince them that your website is worth giving their email.

2. ***An email service*** – AWeber is the most common email service which costs 19$/month if you have an email list up to 500 subscribers. With this, you can send email, set up an auto-responder in which you will thank all your customers who subscribed to you. There are other great email marketing platforms too, such as MailChimp.

3. ***Offer free stuff*** – everybody likes free stuff – books, videos, extras, courses, webinars, tips, a product, etc. You can mention on your squeeze page something like *"Subscribe now and get instant access to my free video course about passive income"*. This is a strategy which a lot of marketers use and which has proved to be effective.

4. ***A sign up (opt-in) form*** – you can use LeadPages, OptinMonster or even free

plugins from WordPress or AWeber's free sign up forms.

It should look like the picture below. Place it in such a manner that your website will look clean and it will catch people's eyes.

Just imagine how would be if you had over 10,000 subscribers to your email list – whenever you have a new offer, a new affiliate product you will send an email to this list and a small part of them will click on what you are promoting.

Email building is crucial for your online success, whether it's a blog, a website, a book, a course, etc.

Whatever you own online, build an email list.

Note – don't send 2 email/ per day or too many emails. People will get sick of your annoying email, and they will unsubscribe very easily. Send emails once or twice a week with relevant content and offers.

Chapter 8: How much money you need to get started and how much money you should expect to make

Website costs

Establishing a niche website will cost you a few pennies, but it isn't expensive.

Domain – The domain and web hosting will not exceed 15$/month.

Content – Outsourcing / hiring a ghost writer to do all the work for you will cost you around $5-$15 /page (landing page). Prices can vary depending on what niche your website will be.

I said $5-$15 because the best length of a landing page/article should be somewhere around 1,500-2,000 words – if you write less, it's a joke and if you write more than that it will get boring for readers.

The perfect article/page size is 1,500-2,000 words. To get an article of that length, a ghostwriter will charge you around $10. You will need at least 10 such pages to start with for 1 website.

You are not allowed to do any kind of e-commerce on that website (which is, in fact, a free blog). By using Wordpress Premium or Business you are allowed to choose a custom domain, a custom theme, to place ads and for the Business plan you have unlimited storage (videos, content etc.). At first, I recommend going for the Premium one ($99/year $9.99/month if you want to pay monthly).

Custom Wordpress Themes – $15 – $100 - if you want your website to be more stylish, purchase a custom domain from http://themeforest.net

Advertising – As much as you want – I highly recommend you to invest some money into Facebook Ads and Google AdWords. As your website will be a new one, it will be very hard for customers to find it, so will need some help at first.

Email marketing service – 19$/month at first – up to 500 subscribers and unlimited emails and it can go up to $300/month if you exceed 25,000 – 50,000 subscribers.

A well-optimized SEO website with clean and relevant content which is also advertised properly will get customers and traffic each month. Don't forget to choose the best keywords.

Let's sum up – you will need somewhere around $130 as a one time investment – theme + content and $25/month for the Wordpress plan and domain/web hosting. In addition, you should invest at least $50/month into Google AdWords and even Facebook Ads.

So you will need $130 initial investment + $90/month.

How much money can you make?

This is a very difficult question.

It depends on the niche, market, competition, quality of your website, how much traffic you get and what kind of products you are promoting. (and how many).

Generally, a well-promoted website with the right keywords and content should bring you from $300 to $1,000 per month on auto-pilot. You only pay the maintenance fees, and you collect your commissions. Occasionally, you need to improve your niche websites and to change keywords, add content, optimize everything and promote it.

Don't forget the cross promotion, promote one niche website on other niche websites and on your blog. Send your traffic from a place to another.

There are websites which generate ten times more income than that. These successful websites have nothing special than what you are willing to build. The only difference is the amount of money the owner has invested in advertising.

It doesn't matter what product you have or what website you have. If it's correctly advertised, people will click on it and will see it. After seeing it, if it's high quality, people will subscribe, buy products and check it periodically.

That's what you need.

Flippa

If you build too many websites or you just got bored of maintaining and updating some of your websites, you can sell them on http://flippa.com and get a 5 or 6 figure deal for it.

There are websites which generate $2,000 to $10,000/month in revenue (not net income), and they sell on Flippa for more than $70,000. You will find there auctions and websites for sale.

In fact, there are people who are building websites, they bring traffic to it, they advertise it, and when it becomes successful they sell it for a lot of money.

Some of them make a living from selling websites. It all depends on the niche of the website, the traffic, and the monthly revenue to make it successful and very expensive for sale.

It's not easy to become successful for every website that you build, but it isn't impossible either. What you need is time, some money and a lot of perseverance!

Chapter 9 – Signing up with Google AdSense

Before you sign up with Amazon, you might want to take advantage of a tool which will bring you consistent money by the time you will be having a big amount of traffic.

This tool is called Google AdSense.

Google AdSense will put on your website ads from different marketers who pay Google to advertise their products/website (via Google AdWords).

You will be paid PPC (pay-per-click) anywhere from 0.02$ to 15$ for 1 click. The price of PPC is based on the website that you have – traffic, audience, content, ranking in Google, etc.

This is a simple process which you can take advantage from and generate additional income from the website that you have already created.

In the future, you are focusing on Amazon Associates program, but I think it's worth signing up with AdSense as you will increase your total earnings.

To sign up with Google AdSense go to http://adsense.google.com and apply.

Chapter 10: Signing up with Amazon Associates – Become an Amazon affiliate

This is the easy part.

As soon as you finish creating your website and everything, all you need is a bunch of affiliate links from Amazon, depending on what you decide to promote.

Go to https://affiliate-program.amazon.com/ and sign up. Make sure you have a valid bank account ID and place everything that Amazon requires.

What you will do at first and what is also one of the most important steps – complete your tax information – you have to sign some papers electronically with Amazon. By signing this, you will notice Amazon if you are a US resident or a non-US resident.

Tax Withholding Rates

Every member of Amazon on any Amazon accounts (including Amazon Seller Central, Amazon Kindle Direct Publishing, CreateSpace, Audible ACX etc.) will have to pay a withholding tax for the US which will be from 10 to 30%:

- If you are living in the US, you will pay 15% of your total royalties/earnings

- If you live in a foreign country which is in tax treaties with the United States, you will pay 10%
- If you live in a foreign country which does not have any tax treaties with the United States, you will pay 30%

Amazon provides a list of the countries which have tax treaties with your country of residence. You may also check your local tax laws, payments, etc. to find out if your country will allow you to get a lower tax withholding rate.

In case you get a 30% withholding rate, but your country will eventually give you an ITIN or Social Security Number for a lower withholding rate, you can modify it at any time by retaking the interview from the beginning.

As soon as you complete the tax interview, and you set up your account, you can start promoting products.

Tools

Amazon will give you some tools to help you promote products on your websites:

1. *Icons and buttons* – you can get from Amazon buttons and icons specially designed for affiliate marketing. You can put those buttons on your website on the left or on the right (recommended), and you can also make them clickable.

2. *Amazon aStores* – you can create an online store within your website. For example, if you choose to promote extreme survival products for your survival (bushcraft) website, you can create an aStore with lots of products in different

categories and subcategories. The aStore is user-friendly and easy to build. You can build the aStore on Amazon and place the link to your aStore on your website at no additional costs. An aStore looks like this:

You can add widgets and custom buttons all over your website, you can make it based on your own methods.

3. *Unique Affiliate links* – Amazon gives you a unique affiliate link for each product that you decide to promote. Remember – you don't have to necessarily sell the product that you are promoting, if you promote an iPad and the customer clicks on the link to the iPad, but he decides to buy an android tablet, you will still get a commission because the purchase has been made through your link and with your help.

Commission Rates

Depending on how many products you sell, Amazon will give you differentiated commissions. The more you sell, the bigger the commission will be. Here's a table with the rates so you can make an idea:

Number of Products Shipped/Downloaded in a Given Month**	Volume-Based Advertising Fee Rates for General Products
1-6	4.00%
7-30	6.00%
31-110	6.50%
111-320	7.00%
321-630	7.50%
631-1570	8.00%
1571-3130	8.25%
3131+	8.50%

The profit margins are exponential as you can see. All of the examples below are based on how many sales you make in one month (30 days).

- If you sell 10 products which cost $50 each, you will get 0.06 x 10 x $50 = $30
- If you sell 35 products which cost $50 each, you will get 0.065 x 35 x $50 = $113.75

- If you sell 200 products which cost $50 each, you will get 0.07 x 60 x $50 = $700
- If you sell 500 products priced at $50 each, you will get 0.075 x 500 x $50 = $1,875
- If you sell 1,000 products priced at $50 each, you will get 0.08 x 1,000 x $50 = $4,000
- If you sell 2,000 products priced at $50 each, you will get 0.0825 x 2,000 x $50 = $8,250
- If you sell 3,500 products priced at $50 each, you will get 0.085 x 3,500 x $50 = $14,875

The more products you sell, the more money you will make and the commission rates will also increase as you see in the examples.

I will cover more in the following chapter regarding which products sell best and how you can find out for yourself if products sell well on Amazon.

Note – you can sell items priced differently, from any categories. As I have mentioned in the previous chapters, you can promote a product, but customers can buy other products through your link, and you will also get paid.

Tip – By promoting a broad niche of products such as electronics – laptops, tablets, accessories, etc. you will get the chance to sell multiple products at the same time. Those products will be expensive too.

For example – you will promote laptops – you promote Windows Laptops, a customer decides to buy a $1,000 laptop through your link, but he also wants a $30 mouse, a $50 bag to carry the laptop, a $30 cooling pad, a $30 protective silicon case and a $40 32GB USB Flash, some adapters priced at $10 and probably an OEM Windows Software priced at $150. Suddenly, from promoting laptops, you might expect a customer to buy all these products within a few minutes and you will sell 8 different products from which you get 0.06 x 1,3$40 (total) = 80.4$ in commissions just from a customer.

The magic is to get as many customers as you can through a good Niche Website or even an Authority Website.

Note – You will get commissions for all those products only if the customer purchases all the products within 24 hours since he/she clicked on your affiliate link.

Chapter 11: Products to promote – how to pick up the best products on Amazon

Criteria

There are several things which you should take into consideration before you start promoting products. Here's a short list of what kind of products you should promote:

1. **Price** – products which have prices over $50, as much as possible. The bigger the price is, the bigger your commission will be if a customer buys a product through your affiliate links.

2. **Demand** – you need to know how long that kind of product will be

searched by customers and how much money you can expect from the product that you promote.

3. **Ranking** – you need to be very careful at what ranking the product has. A smaller rank will indicate that the product is selling good on Amazon. I will cover next how to look at rankings, what rankings mean and what rankings should your products have before you start promoting them.

4. **Quality of the product** – before your promote a product, make sure that it's a high-quality product.

5. **Large variety of related products** – promote products which are related to other expensive products (as the example with the laptop).

6. ***Reviews*** – promote a product which has a large number of positive reviews. If you have a good website and you send a lot of your traffic to products and Amazon, and those products will have poor reviews, you won't get any sales (commissions).

7. ***Availability*** – make sure that the product you promote is available worldwide or at least, on 90% of the Globe. If a customer from Asia clicks on a good product, but that product is available only in the Amazon US store, he will buy neither the product that you promote nor the other related products.

8. ***When the product was available on Amazon*** – it's important to

know when the product was available and here's why – if a product is 3 years old, a lot of the potential customers may know about it or they may have even bought it previously. If the product is relatively new – a few months since it became available, customers will be curious to try it out.

9. ***Popularity of the brand*** – customers like to buy popular products which are also high-quality products. I don't know about you, but when I buy something from Amazon, I make sure that it's popular and qualitative.

Rankings

The ranking of a product is based on how many items the seller sold in 1 day, but ranking also varies based on how many items the other sellers sold in that day. If in one day somebody sells 5 laptops, but the other competitors sell 5-6 laptops, the ranking will remain almost unchanged. Rankings are updating hourly based on sales (orders).

To get the best results, you should promote products which have a ranking below #50,000 in the whole Amazon US Store.

Average Customer Review: ★★★★☆ ☑ (2,967 customer reviews)
Amazon Best Sellers Rank:
    #3 in Electronics > Accessories & Supplies > Computer Accessories > **Keyboard & Mouse Combos**
    #4 in Electronics > Accessories & Supplies > Computer Accessories > **Mice**
Date first available at Amazon.com: July 17, 2011

Note – Rankings or for each store – DE, FR, IT, ES, US, UK, etc. and all of them have individual rankings based on sales. For example – if a product has a #20,000 rank in the US Store, in the UK store it might have #10,000 or #100,000 so you have to check to be sure that it's selling good.

Tip – Promote Bestselling products (Orange Highlights) from different categories. These products are usually, the most popular from their category.

Here's an example for ranking – This DELL Laptop is selling really good, even though it isn't the best selling one, but it hasn't got the best reviews.

ASIN	B00SIJH3TG
Customer Reviews	★★★☆☆ ☑ 38 reviews 3.1 out of 5 stars
Best Sellers Rank	#99 in Computers & Accessories (See top 100) #14 in Computers & Accessories > Notebooks
Shipping Weight	5.6 pounds (View shipping rates and policies)
Domestic Shipping	Currently, item can be shipped only within the U.S. and to APO/FPO addresses. For APO/FPO shipments, please check with the manufacturer regarding warranty and support issues.
International Shipping	This item is not eligible for international shipping. Learn More
Date First Available	January 21, 2015

This laptop is selling well in its categories, I could say that there are over 50 to 100 units shipped every day, it has been recently made available for Amazon, since the end of January 2015. Customers tend to buy other products which go well with the laptop – a mouse, a bag – you will sell a bigger number of products and you will get a bigger commission at the end of the month based on how many products the customers bought.

Frequently Bought Together

Price for all three: $243.48

Add all three to Cart

Add all three to Wish List

Show availability and shipping details

☑ **This item:** Dell Inspiron 14 3000 Series 14-Inch Laptop (i3451-1001BLK) $218.00

☑ AmazonBasics 14 1 in laptop and tablet case $13.99

☑ AmazonBasics Wireless Mouse with Nano Receiver (Black) $11.49

The only bad thing about this product is that it lacks good reviews. If the product had more positive reviews and an overall rating of over 4 stars, this would have been the perfect product to promote on your Niche Websites.

I will give 5 examples of the best possible products which you can promote on your Niche Websites.

Note – it's important to promote only product which fit your Niche Website or the content that you have on your websites. Do not promote products which don't have anything to do with your websites. For instance, don't promote electronics on a Niche Website about Magic Tricks.

Chapter 12: 5 examples of Niches and products you should promote

The following examples are among the most profitable ones – they include expensive products which customers look for. Customers also tend to buy accessories and related products for the ones that they were initially looking for.

Example #1 – Laptops & Accessories Niche

If you have decided to make a Niche Website about laptops, electronics, accessories and other products related to this Niche, you might want to take into consideration writing articles of 1,000 – 1,500 words – reviews, news, impressions, comparisons and put affiliate links to different products on Amazon.

These products can be:

- Laptops
- Bags
- Mice & Keyboards
- Headphones
- USB Flash
- Protective Cases
- Windows Software
- Netbooks
- External Batteries
- USB/Lightning Cables
- Adaptors
- Cooling Pads

As I have mentioned in the previous chapter, customers who click to buy a laptop, will also buy similar products and accessories for their main product, which in our case – the laptop.

Frequently Bought Together

Price for all three: **$1,028.56**

Add all three to Cart

Add all three to Wish List

Show availability and shipping details

☑ **This item:** ASUS GL551JM 15-Inch Gaming Laptop [OLD VERSION] $999.00

☑ Cooler Master NotePal X-Slim Ultra-Slim Laptop Cooling Pad with 160mm Fan (R9-NBC-XSLI-GP) $15.57

☑ Redragon M801 CENTROPHORUS-2000 DPI Gaming Mouse for PC, 6 Buttons, Weight Tuning Set,Omron Micro ...
$13.99

Note – Look in the "Frequently Bought Together" for each product that you want to promote and "Customers Who Bought This Also Bought". You will see exactly where are customers going after they buy the product that you promote.

For a lot of products to promote in this Niche, you might want to build an Amazon aStore as the market is huge.

Customers Who Bought This Item Also Bought   Page 1 of 17

Example #2 – Tablets & Accessories Niche

The tablet industry is constantly evolving and growing – iPads, Android tablets and now even Windows Tablets. Make sure to promote the best ones out there. What you must know is that you have to constantly change products on your website, as there are always new others to come up.

If you have decided to make a Niche Website about Tablets & Accessories, again you might want to promote products like:

- Tablets (Android/Windows/iOS)
- Protective cases – silicon, clam case, bookcase
- Protective shields
- Adaptors
- USB Cables

- External batteries
- Micro SD cards
- Micro SD adapters
- External keyboards
- Parts – displays, battery replacements
- User guides
- Repair guides
- Headphones
- Other related accessories

Make sure to include as many related products as possible. Look for the bestselling products before you review or post articles on your Niche Website to make sure that you will sell.

Example #3 – Photography guides, DSLR Cameras & Accessories

Photographers and enthusiasts, even designers and business people who have a passion for photography, will search the web for new things to learn. You should try to send those people to your affiliate links on Amazon.

You can easily create a Niche Website dedicated to photographers, artists, and enthusiasts – provide techniques, reviews, guides, news on your Niche Website and send the traffic to related products on Amazon.

Products you may consider:

- DSLR cameras
- Mirrorless cameras
- Bags
- Tripods
- Protective cases
- Zoom lens
- SD Cards
- Adapters
- Microphones
- Custom Flash Lights

- Studio Equipment
- Photography Guides
- Manual guides (for cameras)
- Optional rechargeable batteries
- Charging dock
- Cleaning cloths
- Cleaning lotions
- Repair guides
- Buying guides
- Repair kits
- Other

As usual, customers who are looking for a DSLR, for example, tend to buy the camera, a guide, a bag, an SD card and a tripod – these are the most commonly bought items from this niche.

Frequently Bought Together

Price for all three: **$378.93**

Add all three to Cart

Add all three to Wish List

These items are shipped from and sold by different sellers. Show details

☑ **This item:** Nikon D3100 DSLR Camera with 18-55mm f/3.5-5.6 AF-S Nikkor Zoom Lens (Discontinued by Manufacturer) $349.99

☑ 32GB SD Class 10 SCT Professional High Speed Memory Card SDHC 32G (32 Gigabyte) Memory Card for Nikon ... $14.99

☑ Deluxe Soft Padded Medium Bag For Digital SLR Camera Lens & Video accessories Case for NIKON D3000 ... $13.95

#Example 4 – Bikes & Accessories

A lot of people enjoy doing physical exercises, and any kind of sport can be a good niche to go for. For instance – cycling, riding a bike could be a really good niche to promote. Prices for bikes go from $200 up to a few thousands (premium quality) and people also buy accessories. Items to consider:

- Bikes (different sizes)
- Helmets
- Gloves
- T-Shirts
- Shorts
- Sun Glasses
- Water recipients

- Repair Kits
- Brake Pads
- Bike tires
- Bike chains
- Lubricants (for chains)

#Example 5 – Feng Shui Items & Books

Feng Shui is one of the most popular philosophical systems for surrounding yourself with harmony and positive energy. There are a lot of people who are actually looking for objects, books, articles related to this and why I think it's good to promote is because you have a wide number of products which you can promote, and prices vary from 4$ to a few hundred. Products to consider:

- Books
- Ornaments
- Stones
- Jewels

- Paintings
- Other

There are a lot more niches which you can go for – I have just covered a few examples so you can get an idea about what you should be aware of before you start promoting products from a Niche.

Chapter 13: Getting paid from Amazon

Amazon will allow you to track all your sales in a user-friendly dashboard and will give you all the tools you need. At the end of each month, you can view detailed reports with all the units ordered through your links, the number of visitors that you had, the commission rates that you got (based on the number of units ordered -> see previous chapters with the table of commissions) and the amount of money that you earned.

You can get your money in 3 different ways:

1. **Direct Deposit** – Amazon will put all the commissions that you have earned during each month into your bank account. Make sure to provide a valid

USD/EUR/GBP account for a direct deposit. Amazon pays you every 60 days since the report has been released – if you get the report for January you will get paid 60 days since the end of January => At the end of March (or usually at the beginning of April).

Before getting paid, they will announce you with 10 days before payment that your money will be deposited in your bank account on 27-30th of the month.

The minimum threshold for direct deposit is $10, so you will get paid as soon as you exceed this amount.

Note – you will the amount of money that you see on your dashboard (X amount) minus the withholding tax rate that you have initially provided. If you have 30%, Amazon will pay you 70% of what you see on the dashboard.

2. **Gift Card** – you can get your earnings as a gift card which you can use to purchase products from Amazon. The minimum threshold for the Gift Card is also $10. It's recommended to use this if you have got a relatively low amount of money, so you will avoid transfer commissions and fees.

3. **Check Payment** – you have the option to get paid by check but this is a time-consuming method to getting your money.

Note – I recommend you to go for the **Direct Deposit** *method as it is the fastest way to get your money. In some countries,* **Direct Deposit** *isn't accepted by some banks and the only way to get your money is by* **Check***.*

Chapter 14: What you have to avoid

1. **Fake products** – I think this is obvious if you choose to promote products from different manufacturers (a tablet, a laptop etc.) do not promote fake products through you affiliate links.

2. **Forbidden products** – do not promote products which are not allowed or are forbidden (drugs, counterfeit products).

3. **Fake reviews** – do not acquire fake reviews for products because Amazon will see and will delete them. You might also get your account suspended. Also, do not copy reviews from other websites or from Amazon to your product on your website.

4. ***Promote products on other websites*** – do not put your affiliate links on websites or pages that you do not own – it's against Amazon's policy.

5. ***Create only one account*** – Make sure to use only one account as an Amazon Affiliate, having multiple accounts will drive you to account termination.

6. ***Don't redirect your links to other sales page*** – when you send customers to buy a product, you have to send them directly to Amazon and not on any other additional sales page of your own.

7. ***Don't include an affiliate link in a Kindle book*** – this is against Amazon's TOS and you can get into serious trouble – you can get banned from

both Amazon KDP and Associates at the same time.

8. ***Don't include affiliate links in your emails*** – if you managed to build an audience and an email list, keep in mind that you have to avoid inserting direct affiliate links when you send them. This means that you have to send an email with a link to your blog/website and your blog/website needs to contain the affiliate links.

9. ***Don't promote cheap products*** – remember that you only get a small commission which is directly proportional to the product's price. So, in my opinion, products priced under $50 aren't worth the time and effort to promote.

Note – Before you start promoting a product, make sure that you have read and understood all the terms and policies of Amazon. As you want to build and grow an online business with Affiliate Marketing, you don't want to get into trouble in the long run.

Make sure that everything you do is legitimate and correct.

Chapter 15: Tips for optimal productivity and growth

If you want to have a successful business with Affiliate Marketing, you have to take into consideration some aspects which will help and influence your future success:

1. **Set goals** – to obtain what you need and to be focused all the time, you need to set weekly goals, monthly goals, and even yearly goals. This will keep you track your activity and your growth.

2. **Wake up early** – by doing this you will obtain the maximum productivity and have a lot more time during the whole day to focus on your main activities.

3. **_Prioritize your work_** – if you want to succeed, you need to make your online business a priority. Don't listen to people who have a negative influence upon you.

4. **_Read and get informed all the time_** – surf the web (forums, websites, blogs, YouTube etc.) and look for any information that can help you out with your business.

5. **_Get in touch with other affiliates_** – it's important to listen to other people who are in the business and have experience, they could teach you a lot of things and you can grow faster.

6. **_Join seminars, webinars, and conferences_** – go to special events to find out more about your business and talk to other people who are already in

this kind of business. You can always find out new things which can help you out.

7. **Join forms** – every preoccupied person has something to ask. A forum would be an excellent way to interact and ask whatever issues you are experiencing.

8. **Manage your time and money** – this is important for any kind of activity or business that you want to pursue. Make a timetable of your activities and schedule everything that you do.

9. **Take advantage of Seasonal sales** – invest more time and money in advertising during holiday periods (June-August, Easter, Christmas) – people have more money to spend on

items before they go on a vacation and sales will always grow.

10. ***Promote products that you love*** – you will see that you will obtain the best results if you will be promoting products which you have already tested or for which you have a passion. It's easier to review and promote products which you already know. You should promote these at first.

Chapter 16: Final Recap

1. *With Affiliate Marketing, you can promote products on your websites in exchange for a commission.*

2. *Amazon Associates is 1 of the 3 business models offered by Amazon to help you make money online.*

3. *Pick up a profitable niche using a keyword planner and by studying the market and competition.*

4. *Sign up with Wordpress and purchase a plan.*

5. *Acquire a domain and a webhosting service.*

6. *Create content for your website – write it by yourself or hire a ghostwriter to outsource it.*

7. *Optimize your website using SEO.*

8. *Sign up with Social Media platforms to get exposure and additional traffic.*

9. *Start building an email list to get more subscribers and potential customers.*

10. *Sign up with Google AdSense for additional income.*

11. *Sign up with Amazon Associates.*

12. *Complete the tax interview.*

13. *Choose your payment method.*

14. *Start promoting products.*

15. Make money

Other Books By Ryan Stevens

[$0.99 Book] - Online Startup – How To Make Money Online Even When You Don't Have Any

Most startups require money, so to initially make money, start from the bottom. Use the information within this book and use the simplest method to make money online even today.

[$0.99 Book] - CreateSpace For Independent Self-Publishers

Nowadays, people prefer to buy digital eBooks instead of physical ones because it's faster, cheaper, environmentally friendly, and you theoretically have unlimited stock. However, there still are people who prefer physical books and they pay for them even though they're

more   expensive.
You can publish just on CreateSpace or
you can publish on both Kindle and
CreateSpace (I recommend doing both).

Evernote In 90 Minutes Or Less

Not only can you find unlimited ways of
using this app for de-cluttering and
organizing your life, but while you do
that, developers will also find more ways
to improve it and add more features to it.

Express Book Launch

Launching a book on Amazon is a complex
strategy that takes months to be correctly
understood. For most authors on Amazon,
this has been the most challenging
process of the business.

Entrepreneur Enhanced

You don't have to be an expert, and you
don't have to be perfect in what you do;

you only need to be committed to what you do. You have to always push and move on, no matter what happens. Nobody said that it will be easy to become an entrepreneur. "Now" is the right time to get started.

Kindle Publishing PRO

Unlike other books that regurgitate the same information because they're written by inexperienced publishers, this guide will give you the key information from an author who has done it time and time again. Just a few years ago, the idea of publishing a book was far out of reach for most everyone, but with the help of this giant online marketplace, you can quickly and safely publish your own book and make a profit!

More will come up soon, sign up to my newsletter for offers at $0.99 or FREE books – http://entrepreneurenhanced.com

Conclusion

Thank you once again for purchasing the book and taking the time to read it. I hope you found in this book the guide and resources that you have been looking for from the very first beginning.

I hope that one day you are going to be a successful online entrepreneur. I hope that one day you are going to fulfill all your dreams and achieve all the goals that you have set.

Before you go, I kindly ask you to write a review for this book, as it will help me improve my writing style and skills for my future books.

If you have any thoughts or ideas or you want to contact me for any details, please let me know.

More books are on their way, and I will constantly be updating all the books which I release. Any review that I will get will help me improve all my books. Stay tuned for updates.

Thank you,

Ryan

Printed in Great Britain
by Amazon

42423589R00066